D0620889

Prisons

Detecting Bias

Curriculum Consultant: JoAnne Buggey, Ph.D.
College of Education, University of Minnesota

By Neal Bernards and Bonnie Szumski

Greenhaven Press, Inc.
Post Office Box 289009
San Diego, CA 92198-9009

Titles in the opposing viewpoints juniors series:

AIDS	The Palestinian Conflict
Alcohol	Patriotism
Animal Rights	Poverty
Death Penalty	Prisons
Drugs and Sports	Smoking
The Environment	Television
Gun Control	Toxic Wastes
The Homeless	The U.S. Constitution
Immigration	Working Mothers
Nuclear Power	Zoos

Cover photo: Bill Powers/Frost Publishing Group

Library of Congress Cataloging-in-Publication Data

Szumski, Bonnie, 1958–
    Prisons: detecting bias / by Bonnie Szumski and Neal Bernards;
curriculum consultant, JoAnne Buggey.
       p.   cm. — (Opposing viewpoints juniors)
    Summary: Sets out opposing views on the place and value of prisons
in American society, including the issue of fairness to prisoners
and whether prisons can really rehabilitate criminals.
    ISBN 0-89908-604-7
    1. Prisons—United States—Juvenile literature. 2. Critical
thinking—Juvenile literature.   [1. Prisons.] I. Bernards, Neal,
1963– . II. Buggey, JoAnne. III. Title. IV. Series.
HV9471.S98 1990
365'.973—dc20
                                                  90-45284
                                                       CIP
                                                          AC

CONTENTS

THE PURPOSE OF THIS BOOK

An Introduction to Opposing Viewpoints

When people disagree, it is hard to figure out who is right. You may decide one person is right just because the person is your friend or relative. But this is not a very good reason to agree or disagree with someone. It is better if you try to understand why these people disagree. On what main points do they differ? Read or listen to each person's argument carefully. Separate the facts and opinions that each person presents. Finally, decide which argument best matches what you think. This process, examining an argument without emotion, is part of what critical thinking is all about.

This is not easy. Many things make it hard to understand and form opinions. People's values, ages, and experiences all influence the way they think. This is why learning to read and think critically is an invaluable skill. Opposing Viewpoints Juniors books will help you learn and practice skills to improve your ability to read critically. By reading opposing views on an issue, you will become familiar with methods people use to attempt to convince you that their point of view is right. And you will learn to separate the authors' opinions from the facts they present.

Each Opposing Viewpoints Juniors book focuses on one critical thinking skill that will help you judge the views presented. Some of these skills are telling fact from opinion, recognizing propaganda techniques, and locating and analyzing the main idea. These skills will allow you to examine opposing viewpoints more easily.

Each viewpoint in this book is paraphrased from the original to make it easier to read. The viewpoints are placed in a running debate and are always placed with the pro view first.

Detecting Bias

In this Opposing Viewpoints Juniors book you will learn to detect bias. All people are biased in favor of certain things and against others. For example, if you have favorite friends or relatives, it might be very hard for you to find fault with them, even when they do something obviously wrong or unkind. On the other hand, someone you particularly dislike might not be able to do anything right in your view. We do not always see things in an impartial, open-minded way. Our personal observations can be biased by what we like, dislike, or believe. Similarly, authors of books, articles, and speeches are biased in favor of or against a particular point of view. Identifying an author's bias is an important critical thinking skill. Being able to detect the author's bias will help you determine whether the author is presenting an argument in a fair, objective manner or whether he or she is biased in favor of a particular view.

Many times a person's bias will be based on his or her personal experience. For example, a young man who frequently visits the corner 7-11 convenience store notices that the owner appears to eye him with suspicion. The owner may be biased against young people because she believes they may steal items. She may be biased because she has caught young people stealing in her store. The 7-11 owner may have a reason for her bias, but it is still a bias. Many of the young people she eyes with suspicion would not steal.

Now suppose that the owner often expresses her opinion of young people. She suggests that young people are thieves and they are not being brought up right by their parents. It would be wrong to accept the owner's opinion as fact. She is biased. You would have to first understand why the owner says these things before you could evaluate her opinion.

The authors of the viewpoints you will read in this book may also be biased because of personal experience or for other reasons. For example, if an author works in a particular profession, such as in an animal rights organization, she or he will probably be biased in favor of animal rights. Each author will try to persuade you that his or her opinion is correct. In order to figure out whether you will accept the author's opinion, you should attempt to discover whether the author is presenting the case fairly or with bias. Be aware of the author's point of view. What stand is he or she taking on the issue? Why would he or she take such a stand? Does the writer express fear, anger, or other strong feelings when describing his or her position? How do these emotions influence the objectivity of the viewpoint? Does the author use loaded words or phrases, that is, words that are overly positive or negative, to persuade you? Keep these questions in mind when analyzing the viewpoints in this book.

We asked two students to give their opinion on prisons. Both students are biased. As you read, attempt to identify their biases.

I think prisons are cruel and disgusting.

The more I read about prisons, the angrier I get. What person has not done something wrong in his or her life? Criminals are just people who have done something stupid or wrong—they don't deserve to be treated with cruelty. Prisons just make criminals worse, because they think we don't care about them getting better and making their lives better.

One time I accidentally lit a pretty big fire behind our house by playing with matches. It was really stupid. My dad had to put it out. Even though this was really bad, my dad sat me down and explained to me how I could have hurt the family and destroyed the house. He told me how scared he was that I would do something like this. I had already realized how dumb lighting the fire was, and I was also scared. But if my dad had yelled at me, or hit me, or locked me in my room, I might not have felt as bad—I might have wanted to light another fire.

That's what I think is wrong with prisons. A lot of times criminals get locked up in cramped cells, have to eat terrible food, and never get to talk to anyone who could help them. People just put criminals in prison because they don't care about them and don't want to help them. And that's why prisoners just get angrier and commit more crimes when they get out. I think we should have different solutions so that criminals can become more responsible, like I did after I talked with my dad.

I think prisons are fair.

When people argue that we should treat criminals better, I get so mad! Criminals are dangerous. As soon as they get out of prison, they try to hurt and kill people again. How would you like it if your mom or dad or sister was killed and then people said, "Oh, the poor criminal!"

Criminals deserve all the bad treatment they get. The worse the treatment is, the better. Then maybe when they get out of prison they won't want to go back.

My brother Ben is always in trouble. My mom and dad constantly have to ground him or make him stay in his room. They make sure they punish him every time he does something bad. And you know what? I think Ben would be even worse if my mom and dad didn't do this. Like one time I heard Ben's friends telling him to come with them to toilet paper a house. And Ben said no, because he knew if Mom and Dad found out they would ground him again. If my parents hadn't punished Ben before, he would have just gone and papered the house.

Prisons are kind of like parents. Criminals have to have people there to punish them and make them behave. Especially since they have hurt people by their behavior.

ANALYZING THE SAMPLE VIEWPOINTS

Tim and Emily have very different opinions about prisons. Both of them are biased toward a particular point of view.

Tim:

POINT OF VIEW

Prisons are cruel and unfair.

LOADED WORDS AND PHRASES USED TO SUPPORT HIS VIEW

Prisoners live in *cramped cells,* eat *terrible food,* and are *treated cruelly.*

PERSONAL EXPERIENCE THAT REINFORCES HIS VIEW

Tim believes the experience with his dad has shown that punishment doesn't work, so he believes prisons don't work.

CONCLUSIONS

Tim is biased against punishment and prisons.

Emily:

POINT OF VIEW

Prisons are fair.

LOADED WORDS AND PHRASES USED TO SUPPORT HER VIEW

Criminals are *dangerous;* they try to *kill people every time* they get out of prison; people feel too sorry for criminals.

PERSONAL EXPERIENCE THAT REINFORCES HER VIEW

The way Emily's parents have punished her brother has proven to her that punishment works, so she believes prisons would work.

CONCLUSIONS

Emily is biased in favor of prisons.

In this sample, Tim and Emily both express bias when presenting their viewpoints. Based on this sample, who do you think is right about prisons? How might your own bias affect your opinion?

PREFACE: What Is the Purpose of Prisons?

What purpose prisons should serve is one of the most controversial issues in the prison debate. The debate divides sharply over whether prisons should focus on keeping criminals out of society or should be used for reforming them.

Some people, including John Irwin and Rick Mockler of the Prisoners Union, believe prisons must help prisoners reform through education and psychological counseling. These people argue that prisons can and should reform criminals. If prisons were used in this way, criminals leaving them would have enough job skills and peace of mind to find productive work in society. Currently, prisons do run many job programs, as well as high school and college-level classes. But many people argue that these programs are poorly run and too limited to make a difference.

On the other side of the debate are people who believe criminals are not easily changed or reformed. These people point out that many of the criminals in prison today are repeat offenders—they have been jailed and released many times. People who take this view, including Allan Brownfeld, a well-known newspaper writer, argue that the best service prisons can provide is to keep criminals off the street. Money has already been spent on rehabilitating criminals in prison, these people believe, and it has not paid off. Prisons should be warehouses, keeping criminals away from society as long as possible, they conclude.

A critical thinker examining a viewpoint on this issue should be careful to look for the author's bias. An author may be strongly biased in favor of or against the ability of criminals to change their lives. Watch for the biases as you read the next two viewpoints.

Editor's Note: In the following viewpoint, the author argues that prisons should work to rehabilitate, or reform, criminals. If prisons do not attempt to do this, the author argues, criminals will simply return to a life of crime. Follow the questions in the margin. They will help you identify the author's bias.

In this first paragraph you can already identify the author's point of view. Words and phrases such as "ridiculous" and "treating them like animals" reveal the author's bias.

Prisons do not help anyone if they do not reform criminals. It is ridiculous to think that simply locking criminals in prison cells helps society. By treating them like animals, prisons make criminals even more hardened and likely to commit more serious crimes. Prisons must rehabilitate criminals to help them become working members of the outside world.

The public should consider it a moral duty to make prisoners better people. As Warren E. Burger, the former chief justice of the United States Supreme Court writes, "When society places a person behind walls and bars, it has an obligation—a moral obligation—to do whatever can be done to change that person before he or she goes back into the stream of society." It is not right for society to punish criminals without helping them become more productive. Otherwise, criminals have no choice but to turn to crime again.

FEW RETURN TO CRIME		
Type of Crime Committed by Prisoners	Percent Committing New Crimes on Parole	Percent Repeating on Parole the Crime for Which Imprisoned
Auto larceny		
Larceny	22.5	6.4
Burglary	23.4	11.1
Forgery	22.3	10.2
Robbery	19.5	5.1
Narcotics	15.9	10.1
Sex offenders	8.8	2.9
Assault and battery	12.3	3.6
Homicide	5.7	0.4
Other offenses	10.2	3.1
Rates for all cases	18.4	6.8
Number of cases	29,346	29,346

SOURCE: Pennsylvania Board of Parole, June 1, 1946–May 31, 1961.

But rehabilitating criminals is not just our moral duty, it makes good sense. Remember that nine out of ten people now in prison will eventually be let out. If these criminals experience nothing but fear, danger, abuse, and idleness in prison, how do you think they will come out of prison? They will be even more murderous, angry, and vengeful than when they were first imprisoned. As Justice Burger states, rehabilitation is "for our own protection." Releasing prisoners who have been mistreated back into the mainstream of society would be foolish.

The author describes the experience of prison in very negative terms. He is not presenting an objective argument, but rather one that is biased against prison.

Some people say, "But rehabilitation and job training have already been tried, and they have not worked. We shouldn't spend more money on people that have already been proven hopeless." These statements are vicious lies. These are the types of statements that make it impossible to change the system.

Anyone who still believes this idiocy should see what types of "jobs" prisoners hold. Most prisoners are stuck in meaningless, manual labor, such as making license plates, working in the kitchen, or doing laundry. Worse yet, they receive only ten to twenty-five cents an hour for their work. Can we call this rehabilitation? To gain self-respect, prisoners must be given important work with real responsibilities. Prison jobs should also pay the minimum wage. By paying prisoners a fair wage for their work, they will gain new respect for themselves.

What is the author's opinion of prison work? How do you know it is biased?

By giving prisoners jobs, we can begin to treat them like human beings with a future. Right now, prison guards and counselors treat prisoners like children. This rightly makes prisoners angry. Their anger will turn into violent crime when they are released. To prevent this, prisons should offer not only jobs, but someone who cares. Philip Zimbardo, a professor of social psychology at Stanford University, writes: "Reform must start with people—especially people with power—caring about the well-being of others. . . . A prisoner wants someone to care about whether he lives or dies." If prisoners believe someone cares about their future, they may be able to put their job skills to use and lead a normal life after prison.

The main idea of this paragraph is that jobs and caring can make prisoners productive citizens. The author is biased in favor of rehabilitation.

Can criminals be rehabilitated?

The author assumes that criminals can be rehabilitated. Name two arguments he gives for why he believes they are being prevented from doing this. Does the writer express fear or anger when presenting his view? If so, how did that feeling influence his opinion?

VIEWPOINT 2 Prisons cannot rehabilitate criminals

Editor's Note: In the following viewpoint, the author believes that attempts to rehabilitate criminals are a waste of money and time. She maintains that criminals cannot change their behavior. Watch for examples of bias in the author as well as in the people whom she quotes.

What is the author's stereotype of criminals? How might this stereotype bias her views toward rehabilitation?

"Masquerade" is a loaded term. It suggests that both criminals and counselors are merely pretending that rehabilitation might work.

Why might Michael Alston be biased because of his personal experience?

Those who believe prisons can actually make criminals better people have never been inside a prison. They have never heard prisoners laugh at the idea of learning to do anything other than lie, cheat, and steal. Convicted criminals are not nice, innocent people accidentally gone wrong. They prefer the fast life and the good money that comes with being a criminal. Prisons cannot rehabilitate because criminals do not want rehabilitation. Prisons must punish criminals and keep them away from society.

Prison programs that try to rehabilitate criminals are a masquerade. The counselors know it, and the prisoners know it. Counselors just want to keep their jobs, and that means not working too hard to rehabilitate criminals. After all, if there were no criminals, there would be no work for the counselors. As Michael Alston, imprisoned for robbery, says about counselors, "They have no interest in reducing crime. They earn their living off us."

"LOOK OUT! IT'S THE CRIMINAL-JUSTICE SYSTEM! HAR!"

Reprinted by permission of UFS, Inc.

We should not blame these prison counselors for not doing their job. Prison staff do not try too hard to rehabilitate criminals because they know their task is hopeless. It is absolutely insane to trust that criminals will become better people. How do you think criminals became good at committing crimes? They learned to cheat, lie, and sneak. And they cheat, lie, and sneak to get out of prison.

A good example is the case of Willie Horton, a convicted murderer who escaped from a Massachusetts prison while on a 48-hour furlough, or leave. How did this convicted murderer get a leave? Because some idiot believed it would be good for his "rehabilitation." Anyway, while out on leave, he tied up, beat, gagged, knifed, and sexually assaulted two young women. Horton has probably ruined these two women's lives forever. But because some people believed that poor Willie Horton could be rehabilitated, these women had to suffer. Horton could not change. As soon as he was released, he thirsted for crime.

Many criminals cannot or will not adjust to the outside world. Jack Abbott, a convicted murderer and author, writes about repeat offenders, "They keep returning. . . . Almost every one of them feels relieved to be back." Abbot says that prisons become a habit for criminals and that it is fruitless to try to change them.

It would be nice to change violent criminals into good, solid citizens. But experience proves that this is impossible. Prisons should concentrate on punishing criminals so they will not want to commit another crime. Rehabilitation programs are a failure. Convicted murderer and author J. J. Maloney sums it up when he writes, "When all was said and done, none of them worked."

The writer expresses anger at people who have faith in criminals. Expressing anger many times reveals bias. In this case, the bias is that rehabilitation is hopeless.

How might the author make this argument more objective, less biased?

Are criminals hopeless?

Why does the author believe that criminals are too hopeless to be helped by rehabilitation? What are some "loaded" terms the author uses to establish her views of criminals? How do these loaded terms reveal her bias?

After reading the two viewpoints on whether prisons can rehabilitate, make a chart similar to the one made for Tim and Emily on page 8. List each author's point of view, any loaded words or phrases used to support his or her view, and any examples of personal experience (either the author's own personal experience or the personal experience of the people quoted) that might bias his or her view. A chart is started for you below:

Viewpoint 1:

POINT OF VIEW

LOADED WORDS AND PHRASES USED TO SUPPORT HIS VIEW

"ridiculous," "a moral duty,"

PERSONAL EXPERIENCE THAT REINFORCES HIS VIEW

CONCLUSIONS

Viewpoint 2:

POINT OF VIEW

LOADED WORDS AND PHRASES USED TO SUPPORT HER VIEW

"absolutely insane"

PERSONAL EXPERIENCE THAT REINFORCES HER VIEW

CONCLUSIONS

After completing your chart, answer the following questions:

1. How do you think the authors could have made their arguments more objective, less biased?

2. Even after recognizing the author's bias, which argument did you find most convincing? Why?

CHAPTER

PREFACE: Do Prisons Treat Inmates Fairly?

When state-run prisons were first built centuries ago, they were little more than filthy warehouses. Many of them did not even provide enough food for prisoners to survive, even though they had to perform hard labor. Many early prisoners died of diseases related to malnutrition and the filthy conditions they lived in. Since then, many laws have been passed to ensure that prisoners receive decent treatment.

A modern prison serves inmates a varied and nutritious menu. Prisoners are allowed a certain number of private possessions in their rooms, including radios, clothing, food, and books. Many prisons have fully equipped libraries, exercise rooms, TV rooms, and organized activities, such as prison-run newspapers and sports teams.

To some people, including members of the Prisoners Union and others who have fought for prisoners' rights, these comforts are few and unimportant compared to the denial of freedom prison represents. These people believe prisons still dehumanize people, or treat them like animals. They believe society should rely less on prisons and instead use alternatives such as probation and work-release programs.

Others believe prisons are already too comfortable. These people argue that prisoners should be forced to serve hard time. This means no personal possessions or other amenities and no opportunities for recreation. They believe these amenities make prison easier to tolerate, so that prisoners feel that prison is not all that bad.

As you read the next two viewpoints, look for bias in the authors' views.

Editor's Note: In the following viewpoint the author contends that prisons dehumanize prisoners through poor living conditions, overcrowding, and abuse. He argues that prisons should be made more hospitable. Look for examples of bias in his argument.

Can you find the loaded terms in this paragraph? How do they reveal the author's point of view?

Why does the author compare prisoners to rats in a cage? Is this comparison fair and objective? Why or why not?

Prisons are breeding grounds for hatred and violence. Even basically good people become raging animals after spending time in our decaying prisons. Far from being places where criminals can learn from their mistakes, America's prisons are overcrowded, poorly designed, and poorly run.

Prisons are overflowing with far more inmates than they were meant to hold. Many prisons force three people to sleep in a cell meant for two or sometimes only one. If you have ever seen too many rats in a single cage, you know the results of this kind of overcrowding. Is it any wonder that prisoners attempt to kill, rape, and knife each other in these conditions? I know that I would resort to violence to defend my little bit of space. Anyone would.

© Simpson/Rothco. Reprinted with permission.

Many times this overcrowding exists in prisons that are unfit for human beings under normal conditions. Many of our prisons are cold, poorly designed, and completely unacceptable by modern standards. Steve Lerner, a freelance writer who has toured numerous prisons, writes, "At least half of all felons are currently imprisoned in maximum-security facilities built more than seventy years ago, even though many of these institutions have long been judged inappropriate." This is definitely cruel and unusual punishment. We cannot expect to house people under these conditions and think that we are doing them or ourselves any good. Believe me, prisoners' vengeance is boiling to the surface in prisons all over this country, and no one, including your daughters and sons, will be safe from it unless we change our prisons!

What emotion is the author expressing here?

Beyond their cruelty, America's prisons are hothouses of violence. According to Lawrence Greenfield of the U.S. Department of Justice, 779 inmates of state and federal prisons died in 1982. Of those, 357 inmates died from unnatural causes such as murder, suicide, and accidents. Can America truly be considered a civilized nation when over 700 deaths occur each year in its prisons? Prisoners have to fear for their lives in conditions such as these.

Prison guards add to this atmosphere of free-for-all violence. Guards often take away prisoners' free time—the only hours of the day when they can feel free to act like regular human beings. In addition, guards may force prisoners to stay alone in bare metal cells with no bed, sink, light, or toilet, in a practice called "solitary confinement." Jack Archie, a young, bright black man desperately trying to stay alive while serving time in Attica prison, explains that there is "a war" going on between guards and inmates. Should Archie and thousands of others be forced to bear this type of treatment?

What types of loaded words can you find in this paragraph? What bias do they reveal?

Prisons should not be torture chambers for inmates. Society must find a better, more humane way to punish its lawbreakers. We must infuse the system with caring, love, and forgiveness, and we must no longer tolerate this living hell we call reform.

Do prisons breed crime?

What is the author's point of view? Find four words that are used to persuade the reader to accept the author's point of view.

VIEWPOINT 4 Prisons should be dehumanizing

Editor's Note: In the following viewpoint, the author supports the idea that prisons must punish criminals for their crimes. She argues that criminals give up their right to fair treatment when they violate the rights of others.

Do the author's examples prove that prisons must punish? What point of view about punishment do these examples reveal?

How might J. J. Maloney's personal experience affect his opinion of prisons?

Punishing criminals is an ancient practice. Every culture has had a way to make criminals suffer for their crimes. The Old Testament tells of people being stoned to death for offenses such as adultery. In India, thieves' hands were cut off for stealing. In America's Old West, cattle rustling was punished by hanging. These examples prove that any civilization must have a way to punish, and severely punish, its criminals. Severe punishment is the only way to ensure that criminals will not repeat their offenses. It also satisfies society's need to know that wrongdoing will be punished.

Even inmates agree that prisons must be tough to be effective. J. J. Maloney, a convicted murderer, argues that prisoners should not be allowed to work, watch television, place phone calls, or have candy and cigarettes. His theory is that if prisons are boring and uncomfortable, inmates will not wish to return. Maloney believes prisons are simply too pleasant: "Many prisons offer more comfort than the U.S. Army offers its soldiers." And Maloney, who knows the system from the inside, knows a lot more than the so-called experts who believe prisons should be counseling centers.

By Summers for The Dayton Journal Herald

The argument that prisons should be unpleasant is an easy one to make. For example, if you own a pet, how do you make it obey? You usually hit it with a stick or a newspaper, or you holler at it. After you've done this (consistently, of course), the pet usually gets the idea. People are no different from any other kind of animal. Make prisons unpleasant places, and criminals will learn that crime does not pay. As Graeme R. Newman, a professor of criminology, writes, prison should be "like descending into Hell."

Does the author's comparison of animals and humans reveal a bias? Why or why not?

Prisoners should be forced to perform hard labor for long, tedious hours. They should receive no money for this labor. If they refuse, guards should use cattle prods and solitary confinement to make them obey. Any prisoner who commits a rape or murder in prison should be forced to spend the rest of their lives in an isolated cell, with no one to talk to and nothing to do.

People need to be punished. Every parent knows this. If you do not punish a child for misbehaving, the child will do still more extreme and evil acts. Adults also need to be punished. When you punish a murderer by letting him lollygag in prison, serving him three square meals a day, and giving all the comforts of home, do you think he learns to respect another human's life? Inmates need to be punished severely enough to learn to regret their crimes. As Newman states, "Inmates should work off their guilt, and for some not even a lifetime will be long enough. Surely this is not too much to ask when one considers the innocent lives that they have ruined."

What loaded words does the author use to persuade you that she is right?

Severe punishment will not only help criminals; it will help society. The public needs to know that wrongdoers will be punished. Only then can people trust in the system. What good is it to tell your child that crime is wrong if that child sees murderers go unpunished? This is the problem with this country today. By mollycoddling prisoners, we encourage crime. Everyone thinks it is O.K. We cheat on taxes, steal pens and paper from work, and do not tell the cashier when she gives us the wrong change. Let the criminals be punished, and you will see a turnaround in the attitudes of the public.

What is the author's attitude toward most people? Is it biased? How might that bias her argument?

Does punishment deter crime?

Name three loaded phrases the author uses that reveal her bias in favor of punishment. Is the author's comparison of prison to parenting effective? Why or why not?

This activity will allow you to further practice identifying bias. The paragraphs below focus on the subject matter of this book. Read each paragraph and consider it carefully, deciding whether or not the author is biased. Read the statement following the paragraph and select the best answer to complete it.

If you are doing this activity as a member of a class or group, compare your answers with those of the others. You may find that some have different answers than you do. Listening to the reasons others give for their answers can help you in identifying bias.

EXAMPLE: In the United States, more than a half-million people are in prison, and ten billion dollars are spent each year on prisons. Whether these monies are being spent effectively is a subject of great controversy.

The author of this paragraph
a. believes more prisons should be built.
b. takes no sides.
c. reveals a dislike for prisons.

ANSWER: b. The author shows no particular bias toward any side.

1. Criminals must be punished severely for their crimes. Especially criminals who commit violent crimes should never be allowed special privileges, such as weekend furloughs. By showing sympathy for criminals and letting them out of prison early, we show contempt for their victims. I would like to quote one crime victim whose husband was murdered by a criminal who got a weekend furlough while serving time in prison. She said, "I wish I could have a weekend, or one hour, when my husband's death is not on my mind."

The author of this paragraph
a. shows sympathy for criminals.
b. tries to remain objective.
c. shows sympathy for crime victims.

2. Thousands of non-dangerous criminals are being housed in prisons alongside violent criminals. This situation exposes helpless petty criminals to abuse, violence, and even death. The only way to keep these young, basically good people from being harmed is to use alternatives to prison, such as allowing them to work at jobs during the day, returning to prison only at night.

This author expresses a bias in favor of alternatives to prison for petty criminals. Which of the words and phrases used above best shows the author's bias?
a. non-dangerous
b. exposes helpless petty criminals
c. use alternatives to prison

3. Prisons are a permanent part of America's criminal justice system. All societies have tried to isolate criminals from society. In the United States, we use prisons to do this.

The author of this paragraph
a. is in favor of prisons.
b. is against the use of prisons.
c. takes no sides.

CHAPTER 3

PREFACE: What Effect Do Prisons Have on Criminals?

A high percentage of the people serving time in prison are repeat offenders—people who have committed more than one crime and usually several more. This fact is used by people on both sides to support arguments about whether or not prisons promote more crime.

On one side are people who believe prisons are little more than "schools of crime." These people argue that serving time in prison has no redeeming value. It does not prevent people from wanting to commit more crimes. In fact, it does the opposite. Prisoners learn from other criminals new ways to commit crime. And the atmosphere of violence and inhumanity leaves prisoners with feelings of anger and desire for vengeance. As soon as they are released, these people argue, prisoners will commit more crimes.

On the other side are people who believe criminal behavior is part of a person's personality, and going to prison cannot change it. They believe in a "criminal personality," an actual type of person who is prone, maybe from as early as birth, to commit crimes—to lie, cheat, and steal. These people believe prisons can only serve one purpose—to keep these criminal types away from society. Once criminals are released, they are destined to commit more crimes because that is the type of people they are.

As you can tell from the above arguments, each side holds a strong bias. See if you can detect it in the next two viewpoints.

Editor's Note: The author of the following viewpoint believes prisons permanently harm criminals. He argues that prisons promote violence and abuse, leaving criminals with a need to get back at society by committing more crime.

What words does the author use to persuade you to agree with his point of view?

Is the author's opinion of criminals objective? Why or why not?

It is common knowledge that one bad apple spoils the whole bunch; the same is true of prisoners penned up together in a prison. Ask any parent to describe how one "bad seed" in a group of children can make the other children act. It is well known that this one evil child can lead all the others into evil. This is also true in prisons. In prison, we house a few truly terrible criminals with the many others that have committed harmless crimes. These harmless criminals learn even worse behavior from the terrible ones.

Prison conditions help this process. Prisons are boring. They are abusive and full of injustice. Violent gangs wrest control from prison guards and officials and rule prisons with tyranny. These conditions turn minor offenders into violent maniacs.

Few prison inmates perform useful work. The system promotes idleness. While prisoners stand around in the recreation yard, the seasoned prisoners teach the younger ones. They teach them the ins and outs of becoming successful criminals, just as professors

ROTHCO

VADILLO - SIEMPRE, MEXICO

5-29E48

© Vadillo/Rothco. Reprinted with permission.

instruct their pupils. The veterans tell them what type of stores to rob, what kind of guns to use, and how to disguise themselves. One former inmate calls prisons "graduate schools for crime."

Anger plays another important role in creating more criminal behavior. Inmates feel mistreated, and their anger builds up. Once a criminal is back in society, that anger breaks loose, resulting in more crime. According to Philip Zimbardo, a professor at Stanford University, 70 percent of all released prisoners return to prison for committing further crimes. The main reason, Zimbardo believes, is that prisons "are breeding grounds of hatred...a hatred that makes every citizen a target of violent assault."

Zimbardo has done research on the prison environment. Using a group of twenty-four college students, he had half act as guards and half act as prisoners. These were normal, happy, intelligent college kids. He had to end the study after just six days because the "guards" began to treat the "prisoners" too cruelly. The prisoners felt so awful that they were filled with hatred for the guards. And these kids *knew* it was an experiment and that they could stop at any time. How much worse must it be in a real prison? This study proves that prisons breed more crime and hatred.

But we do not need any studies to tell us prisons breed more criminals. Just look at the dangerous youth gangs like the Bloods and the Crips. These groups got their start in prisons. Now they carry their violence through the streets outside prison, murdering and dealing drugs. As Jack Henry Abbott, a convicted murderer, writes, "No one has ever come out of prison a better man."

"I hate to think how we'd have managed if I hadn't learned a trade in prison."

© Punch/Rothco. Reprinted with permission.

Is the author's opinion of Zimbardo's experiment objective? Why or why not?

Is the authors's point about the Bloods and the Crips objective? If you answer no, what would make it more objective?

Can prisons create more criminals?

The author believes criminals become worse in prison. Name three reasons he gives for this belief. Do you think the author makes a good case that prisons have a bad effect on criminals? Why or why not?

The criminal personality is not changed by prison

Editor's Note: In the following viewpoint, the author argues that it is society, not prison life, that creates criminals. She argues that criminals are set in their ways long before they reach prison. Look for examples of bias in her argument.

Blaming prisons for increasing crime is like blaming schools and teachers for their students' poor grades. The theory just does not hold up.

Does the author show sympathy for criminals? How can you tell?

You cannot blame an institution for the way people act when those people have been shaped by earlier and stronger influences. As children, criminals were affected by their parents, friends, television, poverty, and their own level of intelligence. A criminal personality forms long before prison.

Is the author biased toward people who grow up under these conditions? Why or why not?

Budding criminals start young. Their early family life is filled with violence and abuse. Future criminals are children of alcoholics, drug abusers, or unwed mothers. They are victims of divorce and abusive parents. Stanton E. Samenow, a psychologist who first used the term "criminal personality," agrees with this view. He says, "Criminals are criminals, no matter where they are. In prison, their personality remains as it was."

Mike Keefe. Reprinted with permission.

Samenow believes that criminals are people who start out with a bad upbringing but also like and want a life of crime. "A prisoner hears new ideas for crime in prison, but *he* is the one who accepts or rejects these ideas. No one forces him to continue a life of crime.... He is not a victim who is corrupted by fellow inmates. He has made choices in the past and continues to make choices."

Samenow thinks that not all children will turn out to be criminals. It is the children who, at an early age, are known to lie to their parents, cheat neighborhood friends, and torture dogs and cats. These children are simply bad seeds that are destined for a life of crime unless a parent strictly stops their behavior. But most of these children's parents are hopelessly ineffective. The children are let loose to victimize others, and they learn to enjoy it.

Jack Katz, a professor at the University of California, also thinks criminals are born, not made. But he suggests another reason that people become criminals: Some people think crime is fun. He quotes one juvenile delinquent as saying, "We the show people. The glamour people.... Hear people talking about you. Here the bar get quiet when you walk in." Many criminals simply like being feared for their lifestyle.

Other experts claim other factors are just as important. Author David Bazelon believes poverty causes crime. "With nothing to lose, poor people turn to crime for economic survival and a sense of excitement and accomplishment." If a person is poor, a life of crime can be appealing. Poor people want the good life as much as anyone else, and they will resort to crime to get it.

Prisons are not responsible for creating criminals. Society and the criminals themselves are to blame. It is time we realize that criminals are not going to get any better.

How is the author biased toward certain children?

Is the author's opinion of poor people objective? Why or why not?

Are criminals born, not made?

What bias does the author reveal in her attitudes toward criminals? How might she have made her point more objectively? Do you find the author's argument convincing? Why or why not?

Detecting Bias in Editorial Cartoons

Throughout this book, you have seen cartoons that illustrate the ideas in the viewpoints. Editorial cartoons are an effective and usually humorous way of presenting an opinion on an issue. Cartoonists, like writers, can be biased in presenting their opinions. In this activity, you will be asked to detect the bias in the cartoon pictured below.

Harrington/*People's Daily World*. Reprinted with permission.

1. The cartoon above gives an opinion about the U.S. prison system. What opinion do you think the cartoonist has of prisons?

2. Look at the sign at the right of the cartoon, taken from the poem that is placed on the Statue of Liberty. Why does the cartoonist use it here? Who does the cartoonist believe is imprisoned?

3. What other elements in the cartoon reveal the author's bias?

4. For further practice, look at the editorial cartoons featured in the daily newspaper. Try to identify the biases in the cartoons.

CHAPTER

PREFACE: Does America Need More Prisons?

America's federal prisons now contain over a third more inmates than they were originally designed to hold. Thousands of criminals enter the prison system each year. Yet building new prisons remains a controversial issue.

Some criminal justice experts believe new prisons should not be constructed. They would like to see the United States rely less on prisons and more on alternatives. One alternative is restitution—making criminals pay their victims money in compensation for the crime. Another alternative is to place some nonviolent criminals under house arrest. These criminals would stay home and be monitored by an electronic device that would warn police if they left their homes. Still another alternative is work furlough: Prisoners would leave prisons to work in the community during the day and return to prison at night.

Advocates of these programs believe that they are the only way to reduce prison overcrowding. They see building more prisons as an endless, vicious cycle. As soon as they are built, they are filled.

Yet others see building more prisons as a necessary solution to prison overcrowding. Those who support this side argue that the American public does not really want to use alternatives. They feel safer knowing criminals are in prison. Without public support, alternatives cannot work, because people do not want criminals working and living in their neighborhood.

The next two viewpoints discuss whether America needs more prisons. Be sure to watch for bias in the authors' views.

Editor's Note: The author of the following viewpoint recommends building new prisons to solve the problem of overcrowding. This solution would benefit both the prisoners and society, he believes. Watch for words and phrases that may indicate bias.

Does the author treat prisons fairly in this paragraph? Why or why not?

America's prisons are bursting at the seams. Not only are federal prisons overcrowded, they are falling apart. Cracked walls, leaky plumbing, rusting iron, and poor lighting combine to make prisons unfit for humans. Old, overcrowded prisons are hard to supervise, putting guards' lives in jeopardy. Guards shudder in fear as they walk down decrepit hallways, wondering if they will be ambushed. Despite these problems, the public wants lawbreakers locked up. The only way to reduce overcrowding and keep criminals in prison is to build more prisons.

New prisons are also necessary because our courts are putting more people in jail. According to former U.S. Supreme Court

THE RISING PRISON POPULATION			
Year	US population (in millions)	Numbers of Prisoners	Prisoners per 100,000 population
1988	246	582,000	237
1987	244	546,000	224
1983	235	420,000	180
1980	227	321,000	142
1970	203	196,000	97
1960	179	213,000	119
1950	151	166,000	110
1940	132	174,000	132
1930	123	148,000	121
1925	106	93,000	88
1918	92	75,000	82
1900	76	57,000	75
1890	63	45,000	71
1870	40	33,000	83
1860	31	19,000	60
1850	23	7,000	30
1840	17	4,000	24

SOURCE: American Correctional Association

Justice Warren E. Burger, the prison population has more than doubled in the last twenty years. In 1970 there were less than 200,000 inmates behind bars. Now there are well over 400,000. The demand for new cell space, however, has not been met. Instead of building new prisons, wardens have simply crammed more prisoners into the old cells.

Worse yet, judges and others are shortening sentences to reduce overcrowding. So even though the public wants criminals locked up, criminals are getting off with even less time served. Thus dangerous criminals are being let out early to prey on the innocent public. We have to spend more money on prisons. The only alternative is more rape, more murder, and more crime.

How does the author attempt to persuade you that he is right?

The alternatives to prison that some people suggest are untested and ridiculous. No one even knows if some of these programs, like halfway houses, work. Others suggest house arrest. This seems like a pretty ridiculous idea. I hardly think you can trust a prisoner to stay in his house all the time! And what's to stop the guy from making illegal deals on the phone or having his hoodlum buddies commit crimes for him?

Another idea that is doomed to fail is restitution, forcing a criminal to pay money to his or her victim. I hardly think we can trust a criminal to pay back the victim. How would the criminal get the money? Who would collect it? These people do not exactly have good credit.

What is the author's opinion of prison alternatives? How can you tell?

If we stop building prisons, everyone might be tempted to commit crimes. The threat of prison keeps people from becoming criminals. How threatened would you feel if the only punishment for stealing was to have to stay in your house?

We could make prisons better and safer. If prisons were bigger, with more private cells, prisoners would engage in less violence. All people need space. With larger rooms and more area for recreation, I would bet that the level of crime in prison would drop to almost nothing.

The prison system works. The only problem is that there are too many criminals and too few prisons. Building more prisons would be a vote of confidence in the system.

Do prisons work?

How can you tell the author is biased against prison alternatives? Do you think the author's argument is convincing? Why or why not?

Editor's Note: The author of the following viewpoint suggests that alternative forms of punishment be used for prisoners. She does not believe prisons will help solve the overcrowding problem that now exists.

America does not need expensive new prisons. What America needs is a different way to punish criminals. Most people would agree that prisons do not work. They neither scare criminals into obeying the law nor help them change their lives to make them better. Why should taxpayers continue to be robbed to support a system that does not work? They should not. There are many good alternative solutions to the prison crisis.

Alternatives to prison would be a much cheaper solution to the problem than the present one. According to Joan Petersilia, a criminal justice researcher, taxpayers spent close to $10 billion to operate the nation's prisons in 1989. That works out to about $20,000 per prisoner, or more than the cost of a college education. And what is the result of spending this kind of money? A felon spends about thirteen months in jail before being released, unreformed, back into the community. For $20,000 a year, America can do better than this.

Why does the author compare money spent on prisons to money spent on a college education?

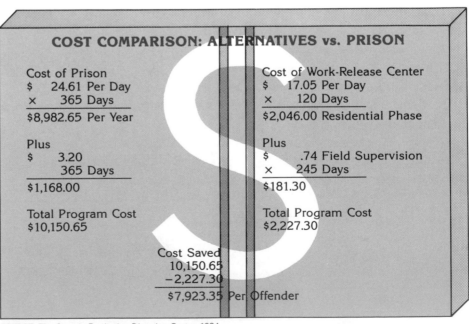

COST COMPARISON: ALTERNATIVES vs. PRISON

Cost of Prison
$ 24.61 Per Day
× 365 Days
———————
$8,982.65 Per Year

Plus
$ 3.20
365 Days
———————
$1,168.00

Total Program Cost
$10,150.65

Cost of Work-Release Center
$ 17.05 Per Day
× 120 Days
———————
$2,046.00 Residential Phase

Plus
$ .74 Field Supervision
× 245 Days
———————
$181.30

Total Program Cost
$2,227.30

Cost Saved
10,150.65
−2,227.30
———————
$7,923.35 Per Offender

SOURCE: The Georgia Restitution Diversion Center, 1984.

One method that would work well is restitution, a plan to force a criminal to pay a sum of money to his or her victim. Charles Colson, who spent time in prison for his part in the Watergate scandal, supports restitution. As he asks, "Why not put nonviolent criminals to work outside the prison where they could pay back the victims of their crimes?" It serves no purpose to lock up a robber or mugger at state expense. The victim gains nothing by tossing the offender in jail. The offender gains nothing by being imprisoned. With restitution, everyone wins. The victim is compensated for the crime committed, and the inmate gets useful work. And the government does not have to build any more expensive jail cells.

What loaded words are used here?

Another option is probation. A prisoner is released after a certain amount of time in prison but is closely supervised. This alternative should be used with nonviolent criminals to allow them to live and work productively outside of prison.

One of the most promising alternatives is to put prisoners under house arrest. This involves placing an electronic bracelet on a prisoner's wrist that can be tracked by police. If the prisoner left home, the police would know. House arrest would be far less expensive than prisons.

And more alternatives could be found. How about forcing convicted drug dealers to counsel kids at youth shelters? How about having people who have committed computer crimes teach people to use computers? Or making people who are guilty of destroying endangered species help enforce the laws in our national parks? The point is that we have to get off our duffs and change this system so it works.

Can prison alternatives replace prison?

What is the author's view of prisons? Is the author's view of how to save money presented objectively? Why or why not?

Detecting Bias in Statements

This activity will allow you to further practice detecting bias. The statements below focus on the subject matter of this book. Read each statement and consider it carefully. *Mark B for any statement that you believe is biased. Mark N for any statement you believe is unbiased. Mark U for any statement for which you are uncertain.* Be sure to provide a reason for your answer.

If you are doing this activity as a member of a class or group, compare your answers with those of other class or group members. Discussing your answer with others may give you a new perspective on your own biases.

EXAMPLE: Clearly, prison systems in the U.S. are releasing prisoners who are obvious threats to society. In one case, a man free on parole was arrested and charged with murdering a New York City police officer. How can we go on thinking about prison alternatives while this goes on?

ANSWER: *B,* bias. While the author may be right to question parole, he does not attempt to make his case in an objective manner. He does not say how many people on parole commit murder.

1. Many prisoners deserve our sympathy and compassion. Some have been abused as children and hated as adults. Instead of being kept in prison, these people could be helped by a caring counselor.

   Answer _____ Reason _____

   _____

2. Prisons are necessary. Criminals must be put somewhere after they commit a crime.

   Answer _____ Reason _____

   _____

3. The criminal justice system is flawed, but it works. For the most part, criminals are punished, society is protected, and sentences are fair.

   Answer _____ Reason _____

   _____

4. Willie Horton had been released on a work furlough when he broke into a man's house, held him captive, and cut him twenty-two times with a knife. When the man's wife came home, Horton repeatedly raped her. The man managed to escape and call the police from the neighbor's house.

   Answer _____ Reason _____

   _____